| WARS OF INDEPENDENCE 1286-1371 | STEWART 1371-1689 | JACOBITE AND HANOVERIAN 1689-1746 | AGE OF REVOLUTION 1746-1900 | WAR + MODERN TIMES 1900-NOW |

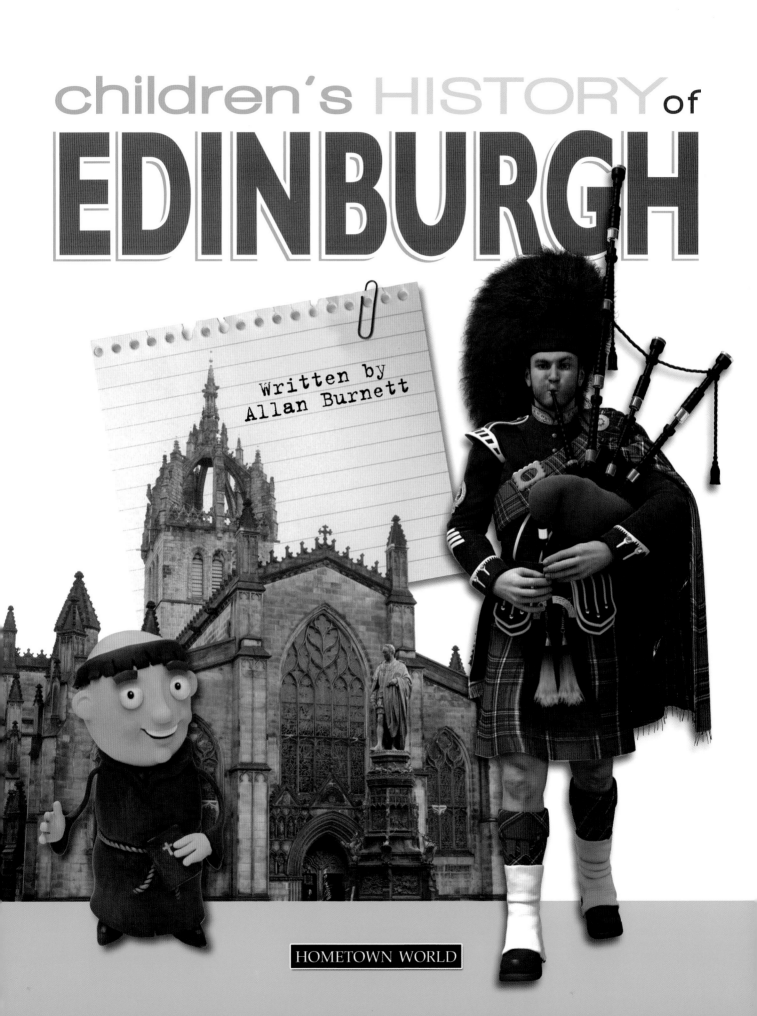

children's HISTORY of EDINBURGH

Written by
Allan Burnett

HOMETOWN WORLD

How well do you know your city?

Have you ever wondered what it would have been like to be a Celt living in a hillfort on Castle Rock? What about being a guest at the Black Dinner in Edinburgh Castle? This book will uncover the important and exciting things that happened in this wonderful city.

Want to hear the other good bits? Some rather brainy folk have worked on this book to make sure it's fun and informative. So what are you waiting for? Peel back the pages and be amazed at Edinburgh's very own story.

Timeline shows which period (dates and people) each spread is talking about

Intriguing photos

THE FACTS

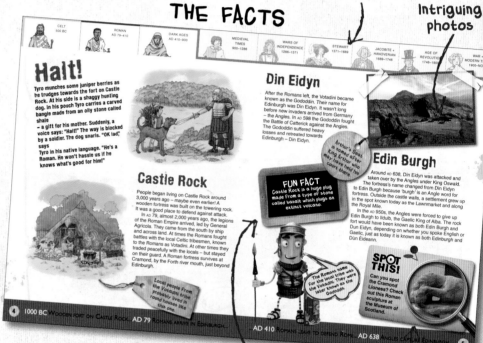

Fun Facts to amaze you!

'Spot this!' game with hints on something to find in the city

THE EVIDENCE

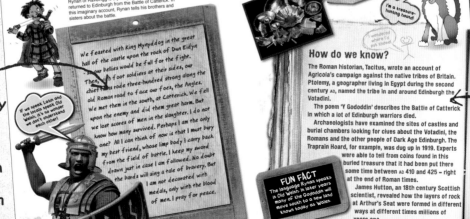

An imaginary account of what it was like for children growing up in Edinburgh

A summary explaining how we know about the past

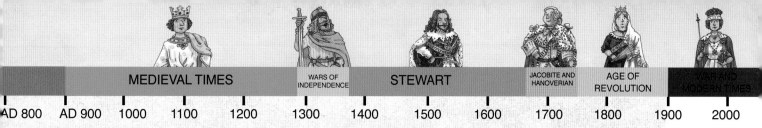

Contents

Halt!

Tyro munches some juniper berries as he trudges towards the fort on Castle Rock. At his side is a shaggy hunting dog. In his pouch Tyro carries a carved bangle made from an oily stone called shale – a gift for his mother. Suddenly, a voice says: "Halt!" The way is blocked by a soldier. The dog snarls. "OK lad," says Tyro in his native language. "He's a Roman. He won't hassle us if he knows what's good for him!"

Castle Rock

People began living on Castle Rock around 3,000 years ago – maybe even earlier! A wooden fortress was built on the towering rock. It was a good place to defend against attack.

In AD 79, almost 2,000 years ago, the legions of the Roman Empire arrived, led by General Agricola. They came from the south by ship and across land. At times the Romans fought battles with the local Celtic tribesmen, known to the Romans as Votadini. At other times they traded peacefully with the locals – but stayed on their guard. A Roman fortress survives at Cramond, by the Forth river mouth, just beyond Edinburgh.

Local people from the Votadini tribe probably lived in round houses like this one.

Din Eidyn

After the Romans left, the Votadini became known as the Gododdin. Their name for Edinburgh was Din Eidyn. It wasn't long before new invaders arrived from Germany – the Angles. In AD 598 the Gododdin fought the Battle of Catterick against the Angles. The Gododdin suffered heavy losses and retreated towards Edinburgh – Din Eidyn.

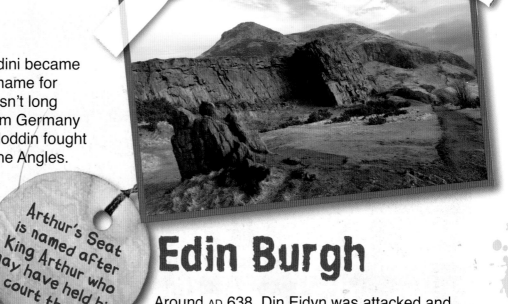

Arthur's Seat is named after King Arthur who may have held his court there.

FUN FACT
Castle Rock is a huge plug made from a type of stone called basalt which plugs an extinct volcano.

Edin Burgh

Around AD 638, Din Eidyn was attacked and taken over by the Angles under King Oswald. The fortress's name changed from Din Eidyn to Edin Burgh because 'burgh' is an Angle word for fortress. Outside the castle walls, a settlement grew up in the spot known today as the Lawnmarket and along the Royal Mile.

In the AD 950s, the Angles were forced to give up Edin Burgh to Ildulb, the Gaelic King of Alba. The rock fort would have been known as both Edin Burgh and Dun Eidyn, depending on whether you spoke English or Gaelic, just as today it is known as both Edinburgh and Dùn Èideann.

The Romans name for the local tribe was the Votadini. They were later known as the Gododdin.

SPOT THIS!
Can you spot the Cramond Lioness? Check out this Roman sculpture at the Museum of Scotland.

Rynan of Ravelrigg is a young warrior who has just returned to Edinburgh from the Battle of Catterick. In this imaginary account, Rynan tells his brothers and sisters about the battle.

If we speak Latin and the locals speak Old Welsh, it's no wonder we don't understand each other!

We feasted with King Mynyddog in the great hall of the castle upon the rock of Dun Eidyn - so our bellies would be full for the fight. Then, with foot soldiers at their sides, our chieftains rode three-hundred strong along the old Roman road to face our foes, the Angles. We met them in the south, at Catterick. We fell upon the enemy and did them great harm. But we lost scores of men in the slaughter. I do not know how many survived. Perhaps I am the only one? All I can think of now is that I must bury my best friend, whose limp body I carry back from the field of battle. I keep my sword drawn just in case I am followed. No doubt the bards will sing a tale of bravery. But I am not decorated with medals, only with the blood of men. I pray for peace.

A hoard of Roman silver was found at the old Votadini capital of Traprain.

I'm a treasure-hunting hound!

I wondered where I'd put those!

How do we know?

The Roman historian, Tacitus, wrote an account of Agricola's campaign against the native tribes of Britain. Ptolemy, a geographer living in Egypt during the second century AD, named the tribe in and around Edinburgh the Votadini.

The poem 'Y Gododdin' describes the Battle of Catterick in which a lot of Edinburgh warriors died.

Archaeologists have examined the sites of castles and burial chambers looking for clues about the Votadini, the Romans and the other people of Dark Age Edinburgh. The Traprain Hoard, for example, was dug up in 1919. Experts were able to tell from coins found in this buried treasure that it had been put there some time between AD 410 and 425 – right at the end of Roman times.

James Hutton, an 18th century Scottish scientist, revealed how the layers of rock at Arthur's Seat were formed in different ways at different times millions of years ago.

FUN FACT

The language Rynan speaks is Old Welsh. In later years many of the Gododdin will move south to a new land known today as Wales.

Queen's Ferry

The ferry is tied up on the south shore of the Firth of Forth. There is a very important passenger on board. Queen Margaret is returning from her visit to the capital Dunfermline. The ferryman's assistant – a young monk – carries ashore cages containing a noisy cargo. There are wild boar and Great Auks from the Isle of May. The boar are for meat, while the bird's feathers will make a fine cushion. Thanks to Queen Margaret, this place will become known as Queensferry.

Malcolm Can-More means Malcolm Big Head!

Big Head

Queen Margaret's husband was King Malcolm Can-More (Malcolm III). Malcolm was a warlike king who killed the old ruler, Macbeth, in battle in 1057. Margaret was a foreigner and a strict Christian. She worshipped a golden cross called the Black Rood. According to some reports Margaret made Edinburgh Castle a more comfortable place to live. She died in 1093, not long after Malcolm was killed in a war against the Norman rulers of England. Queen Margaret became known as Saint Margaret.

A Good Son

King David I was the youngest son of Malcolm and Margaret. He turned the small town that had grown up around the castle into a royal burgh. A burgh was a town made of burghers, or burgesses, who were given land and protection by the king in return for paying taxes. David invited knights from Normandy in France to settle on land around the town.

David also gave Edinburgh its first market charter. The burghers traded goods such as woollen cloth at Edinburgh's market – the Mercat Cross. New silver coins were struck at the Edinburgh mint so that people could trade more easily.

SPOT THIS!

St Margaret's chapel at Edinburgh Castle is the oldest surviving building in Edinburgh.

Mercat Cross was rebuilt in 1885.

David I named Holyrood after his mother's cross, the Black Rood. What a nice boy!

King David's great seal

White Stag

While out hunting one day, King David saw a white stag. Some say David was attacked by the stag. In the struggle, he broke off a cross-shaped piece from its antlers. This was thought to be a sign from God, so David built Holyrood Abbey to mark the spot. The monks who lived there prayed to God, and farmed vegetables and sheep. They employed people to brew beer, make clothes and shoes, dig for coal, and make salt from seawater. Some local lads were taught to read and write.

FUN FACT

Giles is the patron saint of Edinburgh. The story goes that he was shot while trying to save a stag from a hunter's arrow.

...1314 CASTLE BURNS DOWN...1360 THE SHEEP HEID INN IS BUILT...

9

Godron, a young shepherd boy, is resting at the Sheep Heid Inn, near Arthur's Seat. It is one of the oldest taverns in the world. Travellers have been warming themselves at its fire, while having food and drink, since 1360. Now, he listens in as an elderly man tells tales of the Wars of Independence.

Longshanks had another nickname – the Hammer of the Scots.

1372

One windy day in March 1286, King Alexander III left Edinburgh Castle and galloped to the coast. He crossed the Forth by the Queensferry on his way to see his young bride Yolande at Kinghorn, over in Fife. Alas, the king was blasted by a gust of wind and fell with his horse from the cliffs and died! After this the bloodthirsty, long-legged English king, Edward Longshanks, marched north to seize control. Edinburgh was ravaged, Holyrood Abbey set ablaze. English soldiers garrisoned the castle. For many years, Longshanks' son, Edward II, held power in Edinburgh. Finally, in 1314 Robert the Bruce's army blasted the English out of Edinburgh with the help of a local lad called Willie, who led the attack. The castle was burned to the ground and for more than ten years there was nothing up there but a few cows. That was the first War of Independence – but it would not be the last!

Scotland's Lion Rampant was probably first used on royal flags and banners by Alexander II and Alexander III.

Statues of William Wallace and Robert the Bruce, heroes of the Wars of Independence, stand guard at Edinburgh Castle's main gate.

How do we know?

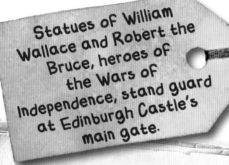

Edinburgh was often attacked by England.

Written documents that have survived from this time can tell us what went on. Rolls of parchment called royal charters granted land to friends of the king in exchange for service or labour. This was called feudalism.

Abbeys such as Holyrood and Newbattle, just outside Edinburgh, trained people to read and write. Some of these people wrote history books called chronicles. The most important is the *Chronicle of the Scottish People*. It was begun in the 1350s by a priest called John of Fordun. Later, a churchman called Walter Bower continued adding to the *Chronicle*. It tells us about life in south-east Scotland from the time of Malcolm and Margaret to the Wars of Independence.

Another important chronicler was Ailred of Rievaulx, an English churchman who began his career at David I's court in Edinburgh. As a way of saying thank you, Ailred wrote lots of nice things about David!

Black Dinner

Robert, the kitchen boy at Edinburgh Castle, is shaking in terror. At the end of the banquet, the head of a black bull is being placed on the table – a sign that the guests will die. Moments before, the Earl of Douglas and his brother were laughing and joking with the 10-year-old King James II. Now James is begging for his friends to be spared. This will forever be remembered as the Black Dinner.

FUN FACT
Edinburgh women were often widowed two or three times because their husbands' jobs were dangerous, especially when they went to war!

Stewart King

The English burned down St Giles and the Town Hall in 1385.

It is 1440 and the rivalry between the royal House of Stewart and the Douglas Clan has come to a head. Why? Because the Scottish court saw the young 6th Earl of Douglas as a threat to the 10-year-old King James II. So he was murdered in cold blood.

The Stewart kings needed to protect their throne. In 1507, King James IV ordered the construction of a great galleon at Newhaven. The warship, called the *Great Michael*, was launched in 1512. It was twice the size of the English King Henry VIII's biggest ship, the Mary Rose.

The *Great Michael* had four masts, about 60 guns and more than 1,000 sailors.

Printing Press

Before the printing press, books had to be laboriously hand-written one at a time. Now, on the printing press, they could be produced in their thousands. It was a revolution. With James IV's permission, Scotland set up its first printing press around 1508 in the Cowgate. Two men called Andrew Myllar and Walter Chepman bought a press, metal type, inks, paper and binding material. They were soon printing books about the same size as a handheld games console – perfect for easy reading or carrying in your pocket. Some people didn't approve of books. They thought printed books contained dangerous ideas.

SPOT THIS!

Can you spot Mons Meg cannon in Edinburgh Castle? It's one of the biggest medieval guns ever made.

A map of Edinburgh around 1500

Around 12,000 people lived in Edinburgh by 1500.

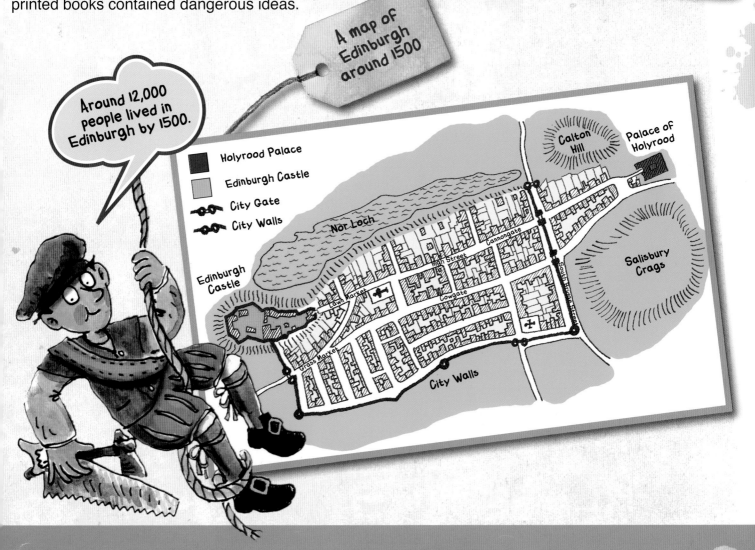

Holyrood Palace
Edinburgh Castle
City Gate
City Walls

Nor Loch
Calton Hill
Palace of Holyrood
Salisbury Crags
Edinburgh Castle
High Street
Cannongate
South Bridge Street
Lawn Market
Cowgate
Grass Market
City Walls

Protest!

Maggie sits with her dad in the cart as the horse clip-clops down the busy Royal Mile. The warm August air makes the animal skins in the cart smelly. They are delivering them to the port at Leith. But there's trouble ahead. An angry mob is shouting insults about Queen Mary and the Church, and heading towards the palace.

The lantern tower was added to St Giles Cathedral in 1490.

Fiery Preacher

In the 1500s, Edinburgh grew bigger. The capital city was now the place to do business. The Cowgate, below the Royal Mile, was a busy street where animals were butchered and their hides sold to make clothing, shoes and belts. Edinburgh people became wealthy and better educated.

John Knox was a fiery preacher at St Giles Cathedral. He wore black robes, a hat, and a long beard. He wanted to reform, or change, the Catholic cathedral. The Reformers' religion was Protestantism. By 1560, the Reformers had support in high places. Catholic statues were taken from St Giles and plopped into the murky Nor Loch, where Princes Street Gardens is now. They were not wanted. This period of time was called the Reformation.

After Knox died it is said his breeches (trousers) were turned into a cap and given to Edinburgh University. Over 400 years later, this cap is still tapped on the heads of university students when they graduate.

Queen in Disguise

Not everyone wanted to become a Protestant. The most important Catholic in Edinburgh was Mary, Queen of Scots. Born in Scotland, Mary grew up in France. She returned to Edinburgh in August 1561, but was hounded by Protestants. To outfox them Mary went around Edinburgh disguised as a man, entering shops where women were forbidden. The Protestants murdered Mary's servant David Rizzio right in front of her, while she was pregnant with her son – the future James VI. Later, Mary's husband Lord Darnley was assassinated. The queen had to flee.

Wasnae me missus!

FUN FACT
People drank a lot of beer in Edinburgh in the 1500s, because the water was too dirty. Brewing was mostly done by widows.

John Knox may have lived at the Netherbow before he died.

Teenage King

When King James VI was thirteen he made a grand entry into Edinbugh and lived at Holyrood Palace. He founded Edinburgh University three years later, in 1582. He hunted animals – and witches, too!

SPOT THIS!
Cowgate was a long street through which cows and sheep were herded to be sold at town markets.

In 1563 the Witchcraft Act made witchcraft punishable by execution. This letter is an imaginary account from the 1590s written by Geordie, a servant lass who works in a grand house on the Lawnmarket near Edinburgh Castle.

Some men were also accused of witchcraft, too.

1592

They burned another witch up on Castle Hill yesterday. You could smell it all the way down the High Street. They say she stuck needles into a wee wax doll of King James to try to curse him. Plus she made her cat talk. Now that isn't natural! I also heard that she was really an honest woman who was good at healing. She used herbs and whatnot to make lotions. It was only when they made her stop trying to heal people that she got angry at the king. They said she was in league with the Devil, even though she was a Christian. Anyway, now the witch is gone but she has a daughter who is the same age as me. My lord and lady want to take her in, but I suppose it will be up to the Kirk or the king to decide what happens to her. Poor soul.

The word "Kirk" is a Scots word for the Protestant Church

The Heart of Midlothian marks the spot where the Tolbooth once stood.

FUN FACT
Before being executed, witches were locked in the Tolbooth – which is also where the town council met!

Hundreds of witches were burned outside Edinburgh Castle. Witches' Well marks the spot today.

There were 8,000 adults living in Edinburgh in the 1590s.

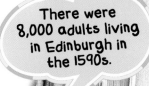

How do we know?

The Burgh records tell us that the town was getting a lot bigger and busier during the 1500s. These records tell us how people lived, and what jobs they did, such as metalworking or shopkeeping.

Historians such as Andrew of Wyntoun, John Mair and Hector Boyce chronicled events in Edinburgh. Another source is the court poets, known as Makars, such as William Dunbar.

The History Of The Reformation In Scotland written by the preacher, John Knox, records his view of events. Mary, Queen of Scots, wrote lots of letters which tell us a bit about what she thought of Edinburgh. The parliament and the privy council which ran things and met mostly in Edinburgh, also kept records. They tell us a lot about the witch trials and were responsible for the Witchcraft Acts. King James VI wrote a book about witchcraft, too, published in 1597. It was called 'Demonologie'.

Jenny Geddes

The bishop begins reading, and people groan and roll their eyes. This English ceremony sounds to Scottish ears too much like the old Catholic Mass they had got rid of during the last century. Suddenly, a woman called Jenny Geddes stands up and shouts at the minister: "Daur ye say Mass in my lug?" (Hint – lug is an old Scots word for ear.) She picks up her prayer stool and hurls it at the hapless churchman. A riot breaks out – and there will be worse to come.

National Covenant

It is 1637. The congregation in St Giles Cathedral wait with bated breath to see whether the Bishop of Edinburgh will use the new English prayer book.
Since the Union of the Crowns between Scotland and England back in 1603, King James VI of Scotland, who was also James I of England, went to live in London. Now his son, Charles I, has annoyed the Scots by trying to make them more like the English – using his loyal bishops to try to make Scottish church services more like English ones. Many Scots refused to do as they were told.
In 1638, people gathered in Greyfriars Kirkyard to sign up to The National Covenant. This document was a warning to the King that he should leave the Scottish Church alone – or else!
Charles I ignored the National Covenant. It eventually led to bloody civil war across Britain and Ireland.

Greyfriars Kirkyard was once a herb garden growing plants for making medicines.

FUN FACT
Old Parliament Hall is hidden behind a fake wall, complete with false windows. Go to Parliament Square next to St Giles and take a close look!

Plague

In 1644, the plague came to Edinburgh, spread by flea bites.

The plague doctor, George Rae, dressed in leather and wore a mask to protect against 'bad air'.

The fleas lived on black rats that nested on ships travelling in and out of Edinburgh's Port of Leith. A large number of Edinburgh people died. To control the spread of the disease, people were put in quarantine, meaning they had to stay at home, or were taken to huts in fields outside the town such as Sciennes. Some Covenanters said the plague was a punishment from God. One of the areas said to have been hit by the plague is Mary King's Close, which today lies hidden beneath the City Chambers.

Headless Heroes

There is a copy of the National Covenant in the National Library.

Woo! I'm a ghost!!

Two famously grisly executions took place at this time. One was of the Marquis of Montrose, the other of the Marquis of Argyll. Both supported the National Covenant against Charles I. Later, Montrose switched sides to support the king. Civil war broke out. The daring Montrose won battles against the Covenanters but Charles I was executed – by the English! Montrose was hanged in May 1650 on the High Street and his head was put on a spike at the Tolbooth.

As for the Marquis of Argyll, he was against Charles I, so in 1661, after King Charles II was restored to the throne, Argyll got his head chopped off and skewered on the Tolbooth just like his friend-turned-foe Montrose.

SPOT THIS!

Can you spot a list of names of the original Covenanters? Check Greyfriars Kirkyard.

GREYFRIARS CHURCH THE NATIONAL COVE
ND SIGNED 28ᵗʰ FEBRUARY 1638. IN THE CHUR
F HISTORICAL INTEREST SUCH AS THE MA
OWARDS THE NORTH EAST AND THE COVE
OWARDS THE SOUTH WEST ALSO THE G
OTSMEN AND CITIZENS OF EDINBUR
OF THE MOST IMPORT
DOUGLAS   EARL OF MORTON R
UCHANAN   HISTORIAN A
ENDERSON   CHURCHMAN
ENZIE   KING'S

The Union

Thomas is a musician at St Giles Cathedral. Today is 1 May, 1707. The people of Edinburgh are meant to be celebrating the marriage of Scotland and England – the Union that has created Great Britain. But few people are happy. Thomas strikes the keys that will ring the bells. The bells of St Giles play the tune, 'Why should I be so sad on my wedding day?'

Fresh Water

Shame

Most Scottish people didn't support the Union because it closed the Scottish Parliament. Decisions about Scotland would be made by the English Parliament. But one family in Edinburgh was celebrating the Union. The Duke of Queensberry was away partying in London, where he had just helped to make sure the Act of Union was passed. Back home, his eldest son James decided to have a little celebration of his own. The trouble was, James was a violent maniac normally kept under lock and key. On this day he somehow escaped and murdered one of the servants – then roasted the body on a spit in the kitchen. Some folk said this shameful act was a punishment for James's father supporting the Union.

Edinburgh's nickname was 'Auld Reekie' because it had open, smelly sewers!

In 1720, a big wooden pipe was laid to carry water to wellheads on the Royal Mile. The city's water supply had opened back in the 1680s, but it was not great. Now it would satisfy many thousands more people. Fresh drinking water was vital to good health, and people came to collect it from the wellheads in special narrow buckets called stoups. Another major health improvement came in 1729, when the city opened its first hospital – the Edinburgh Royal Infirmary.

FUN FACT
The world's first golf club was founded in Edinburgh in 1744. It was called The Honourable Company of Gentlemen Golfers.

Maggie Dickson

In 1724, a young fish-seller called Maggie Dickson was accused of murdering her child. Maggie was innocent, but the judge did not believe her. She was hanged in the Grassmarket. Her body was taken away by horse-drawn carriage to be buried. When the carriage went over a bump, Maggie woke up. The hangman's noose had not killed her after all. She could not be executed twice, so she was freed. She had many children and forever after was known as 'Half-hangit Maggie'.

The stone-built Canongate Tolbooth survived the great Fire of 1700.

Riots

John Porteous was the captain of the city guard, the policemen of their day. When a smuggler was executed in 1736, a riot broke out. Porteous ordered his men to fire at the mob to restore calm – many people were killed. Porteous was sentenced to death for ordering the shootings but then let off. The Edinburgh mob were outraged. So they broke into the Tolbooth jail, dragged Porteus out and hanged him on the spot. This was mob rule!

SPOT THIS!

Can you spot this wellhead on the Royal Mile? Wells built in Edinburgh around 1675 improved the town's water supply.

During the 1700s, the population of Edinburgh doubled to almost 100,000!

Bonnie Prince

Thousands of people greeted Bonnie Prince Charlie when he arrived in Edinburgh in September 1745. His mission was to win back the crown for his family, the Stewarts. Charlie set up court in Holyrood Palace and charmed the local ladies, but failed to capture Edinburgh Castle. Charlie was defeated the following year.

All Change!

I grasp Grandfather's hand as the steam train makes a loud hiss and blasts its whistle. The smell of coal smoke and grease from the train is so strong! Grandfather says the smell reminds us of what it must have been like here long ago. This spot was home to a foul-smelling sewer called the Nor Loch. They had to drain the loch to build railway platforms in this valley under the castle. Suddenly, the conductor shouts: "All aboard!"

The New Town

People were fed up with living in the smelly Old Town, or 'Auld Reekie'. So, in 1766, a competition was held to design the New Town. The winner was a young architect called James Craig. The New Town was built on fields on the north shore of Nor Loch, which was drained and eventually turned into Princes Street Gardens and Waverley Station. A new stone bridge, North Bridge, connected the Old Town with a New Town.

James Craig's First plan of New Town 1768.

Birthday Riot

A protest on 4th June, 1792, King George's birthday, ended in a riot. Some people in Edinburgh were protesting about the way they were being governed. They wanted to get rid of the royal family. The rioters burned a straw dummy of Robert Dundas, who governed Scotland, and attacked his house. King George sent in the army to stop the riot and at least one person was shot and killed.

Thinkers and Writers

The University and coffee shops of Edinburgh were full of people swapping bright ideas and discussing new ways of doing things. The philosopher David Hume argued that there was no such thing as heaven. His friend, Adam Smith, wrote a book called *The Wealth of Nations*. Their books and articles began to change the way people thought. Science was thriving in Edinburgh too. James Craig designed an observatory on Calton Hill. Astronomers could view the stars through its new telescope.

The Scott Monument was built in the 1840s in honour of the novelist Sir Walter Scott.

FUN FACT
Princes Street only has buildings on the north side because when the New Town was built residents wanted to keep their view of the castle.

Medical Matters

The Edinburgh Medical School inspired doctors – and writers. The author Arthur Conan Doyle based his Sherlock Holmes detective character on an Edinburgh doctor called Joseph Bell. Robert Louis Stevenson wrote a tale called 'The Body Snatcher'. It was based on real-life Edinburgh murderers and grave-robbers Burke and Hare. They took bodies to Surgeon's Square where Dr Knox dissected them in anatomy lessons!

I'm not a grave robber – I'm a scientist!

Outbreaks of the deadly disease cholera provided a regular supply of bodies for dissection!

SPOT THIS!
Can you spot a statue of Sherlock Holmes near the place where Sir Arthur Conan Doyle once lived?

This imaginary account was written by a gentleman traveller. He was born in Edinburgh and now returns to visit the city as a grown-up in 1868. He describes how Edinburgh has changed and what is still the same.

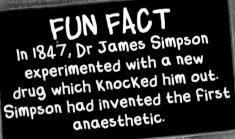

These new McVitie's biscuits are delicious.

FUN FACT
In 1847, Dr James Simpson experimented with a new drug which knocked him out. Simpson had invented the first anaesthetic.

Even before I got off the steam train, I saw that Edinburgh was changing. Workmen are turning the three separate railway stations here into one big station. It will be called Waverley Station. When I was born, there was no railway here at all, just a foul-smelling open sewer called the Nor Loch!

I left the station. High up above me was the Castle Rock, where a fortress has stood for more than a thousand years.

I walked through pretty Princes Street Gardens to Speaker's Corner on the Mound. A young woman was making an angry speech demanding that women should be allowed to vote.

There are two magnificent new buildings — the Royal Scottish Academy and the National Gallery. The High Street was busy. There were still horse-drawn carts, errand boys, shops and stalls as I remember them, so in some ways Edinburgh hadn't changed.

...1892 DIGESTIVE BISCUIT INVENTED IN EDINBURGH...

The railway station is named after one of Scott's books, Waverley.

The new Jenners store of 1895 was very modern, with electric lights and lifts!

How do we know?

In 1849, George Bell wrote a book called *Day And Night In The Wynds of Edinbugh*. He describes the drunks in the Lawnmarket at the top of the Royal Mile:

'Four grown lads were wrestling each other by way of amusement, and roaring out the most shocking obscenities and most fearful blasphemies – from the toothless infant to the toothless old man the population of the wynds drinks whisky.'

From the 1850s onwards, cameras became more common, and old photographs provide a fantastic record of what Edinburgh looked like.

This is a Victorian camera. The leather bellows were moved in or out to change the focus.

Sophia Jex-Blake became Britain's first female medical student at Edinburgh in 1869.

VOTES FOR WOMEN

At War!

Grace tucks her wee brother Davie into a makeshift bunk bed. They are in a huge, dark tunnel. It is filled with people in beds or huddled by the walls. A man in uniform stands by a sign: 'Warden Post No.4'. Davie asks where his daddy is. He was working when the air-raid siren went off. Just then, they hear a voice they recognize. It's dad. "Thank goodness I've found you two!" he says.

The War Years

The men of the Royal Scots were no strangers to war – it was the oldest regiment in the British Army. During World War One they were commanded by General Douglas Haig. He came from Edinburgh and there is now a statue of him at the Castle. The war with Germany ended in British victory, but around 12,000 men from the Royal Scots were killed.

When World War Two broke out in 1939, many children from Edinburgh were evacuated from their homes to live in the countryside where it was safer from attack. Anyone who stayed in Edinburgh had to find a shelter when the air-raid sirens sounded. The sirens meant that enemy aircraft were on their way to drop bombs on the shipyards and docks. In 1940 a stray bomb hit the zoo, killing a giraffe. By the end of the war in 1945, 18 people had been killed in air raids.

World War One memorial in Princes Street Gardens.

FUN FACT

More than 140,000 people went to see Buffalo Bill's Wild West Show in a field at Gorgie, on the west side of Edinburgh, in 1904.

Festivals

After the World Wars, people wanted a bit of fun to lift the gloom. In 1947, the first Edinburgh International Festival was staged. Companies from outside Scotland were invited here to perform classical music, theatre and ballet. That same year, the Edinburgh Fringe Festival was set up so that a wider range of people could perform. The Fringe is now the biggest arts festival in the world. The festivals were followed in 1950 by the first Edinburgh Military Tattoo at the Castle, where Scottish pipe bands are joined by performers from around the world to entertain huge crowds. Did you know that Edinburgh actually hosted an early kind of festival back in 1814?

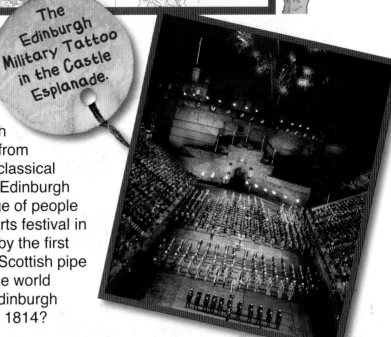

The Edinburgh Military Tattoo in the Castle Esplanade.

All Change!

In the 1930s, nine out of ten Edinburgh workers were paid less than £10 a week.

In 1956, there were some big changes in Edinburgh. A new, modern home for the National Library of Scotland was opened on George IV Bridge. It is home to more than seven million books. An even more noticeable change was the end of the trams. Horse-drawn trams running on iron rails had been around since the 1800s. These were replaced by cable trams and then electric trams. In 1956, buses took over. To this day, many city buses still follow the same routes as the trams and have the same numbers. Since then, there have been schemes and plans to make trams the future again!

National Library of Scotland

SP☉T THIS!

Can you spot this plaque to the actor Sean Connery who was born in Fountainbridge in 1930?

Commemorating the Centenary of Cinema

SEAN CONNERY
*Born Fountainbridge
(25th August 1930)
Oscar Winning Actor
International Film Star*

The Scottish Film Council

Today and Tomorrow

Edinburgh has come a long way since the Romans arrived 2,000 years ago. We know how it has changed thanks to objects dug from the ground, written records, old maps and paintings and the many historical buildings that survive. So how will people know about today's Edinburgh folk in the future?

⬆ Edinburgh Zoo on Corstorphine Road is home for squirrel monkeys, penguins and many other wild animals.

You should feel proud to be part of Edinburgh's future!

⬆ The one o'clock gun has been fired from the Mills Mount Battery at Edinburgh Castle since 1861. It used to mark the time for ships in the Firth of Forth. Today, visitors to Edinburgh enjoy the spectacle.

⬅ The Scottish Parliament opened at Holyrood in 2004. This is where new laws are made that change the lives of everyone living in Scotland.

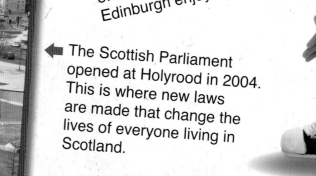

FUN FACT
Edinburgh has three football teams: Heart of Midlothian FC, Hibernian FC and Edinburgh City FC.

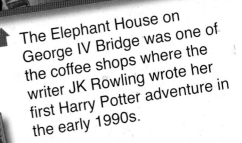

the elephant house

The Elephant House
"Birthplace of Harry Potter"
New web site
www.elephanthouse.biz

You can find out about Edinburgh's famous authors at the Writers' Museum. Do you know anyone who might become a famous writer in the future? ➡

THE WRITERS' MUSEUM

⬆ The Elephant House on George IV Bridge was one of the coffee shops where the writer JK Rowling wrote her first Harry Potter adventure in the early 1990s.

You can see the whole of Edinburgh through a periscope in the Camera Obscura on Castle Hill.

⬅ Our Dynamic Earth will take you back millions of years to discover Edinburgh's volcanic past – it's hot stuff!

How will they know?

How will future generations know what Edinburgh was like for us, now? The internet is a great way of recording the present. Photos, blogs and stories from tourists can all spread the word about our wonderful coastline and countryside. Hundreds of years from now someone may be looking at your picture or reading your blog. You're making history!

29

Glossary

Abbey – a building where monks or nuns live and work. An Abbot is in charge of monks, an Abbess is in charge of nuns.

AD – a short way to write anno Domini, which is Latin and means 'in the year of Our Lord', i.e. after the birth of Christ.

Air raid – during World War Two, sirens sounded to warn people that enemy planes were coming to drop bombs. People hid inside air-raid shelters.

Anatomy – the scientific study of the structure of plants, animals and humans.

Archaeologist – a person who studies the past by examining buildings and objects left behind by previous people and cultures.

Bard – a Celtic poet who recites long poems about the great adventures of their tribesmen.

Cargo – goods carried by a ship, plane or other vehicle.

Catholic – or Roman Catholic: a member of the Christian religion who considers the Pope its head.

Charter – written permission to do something. It is often a Royal Charter, meaning the king or queen has given permission.

Chieftain – the head of a clan or tribe.

Cholera – a deadly disease caused by filthy water.

Christian – one who believes Jesus Christ is the son of God, and follows his teachings.

Christianity – the name of the religion whose followers believe Jesus Christ is the son of God.

Civil war – a war where people in the same country fight each other.

Dark Ages – a period of time in history, roughly between the late 5th century AD and the 10th century AD.

Dissect – cut something open and examine it, usually dead plants, animals or people.

Evacuate – having to leave your home and live somewhere else for safety.

Friars – male members of the Roman Catholic religion. There were Grey Friars, White Friars, Black Friars and Austin Friars.

Garrison – where soldiers stay while they are guarding a place.

Latin – the language of ancient Rome and the foundation of many other languages.

Legion – a military unit in the Roman army of between 3,000 to 6,000 men.

Monastery – a place where monks live and worship.

Monk – a male member of a religious community that has rules of poverty, chastity and obedience.

Plague – a disease that spreads easily and can kill. In medieval times, it was also called the Black Death.

Pope – the official name for the head of the Roman Catholic Church. The Pope lives in the Vatican in Rome.

Protestant – a member of the Christian religion who considers the king or queen of England to be the head of its church.

Seal – an image pressed in wax to seal a document or letter. An unbroken seal showed that the document was official and had not been opened.

Index

Acknowledgements

The publishers would like to thank the following people and organizations
for their permission to reproduce material on the following pages:

p5: BCS/Alamy; p7: National Museums of Scotland; p9: Kim Traynor/Wikipedia; steel engraving from *The Pictorial History of Scotland*/Wikipedia; p22: Geographicus Rare Antique Maps/Wikipedia; p23: Kim Traynor/Wiki; p25: Swindon Museum; p27: The Royal Edinburgh Military Tattoo; p28: Edinburgh Zoo; p29: Yerbury Photography/Alamy

All other images copyright of Hometown World

Every effort has been made to trace and acknowledge the ownership of copyright.
If any rights have been omitted, the publishers offer to rectify this in any future editions.

Written by Allan Burnett
Educational consultant: Neil Thompson
Local history consultant: Mark Jardine
Designed by Sarah Allen

Illustrated by Kate Davies, Dynamo Ltd, Virginia Gray, Tim Hutchinson,
Peter Kent, Leighton Noyes, Nick Shewring and Tim Sutcliffe

First published by HOMETOWN WORLD in 2011
Hometown World Ltd
7 Northumberland Buildings
Bath BA1 2JB

www.hometownworld.co.uk

Copyright © Hometown World Ltd 2011

ISBN 978-1-84993-208-0

CELT	ROMAN	DARK AGES	MEDIEVAL TIMES
500 BC	AD 79-410	AD 410-900	900-1286